Snails in School!

Contents

Christine Economos

Today the snails came.

We will learn about them.
We can't wait!

Our snails will live in boxes.
We need to make
good homes for them.

We put in dirt.
We put in rocks.
We put in twigs.

Will the snail come out?
I put a little water near it.
Nothing happens.

I blow on it gently.
A little head pops out.

I see four tentacles.
I see two tiny eyes.
I think the snail is looking at me!

I draw what I see.
I name the parts of my snail.

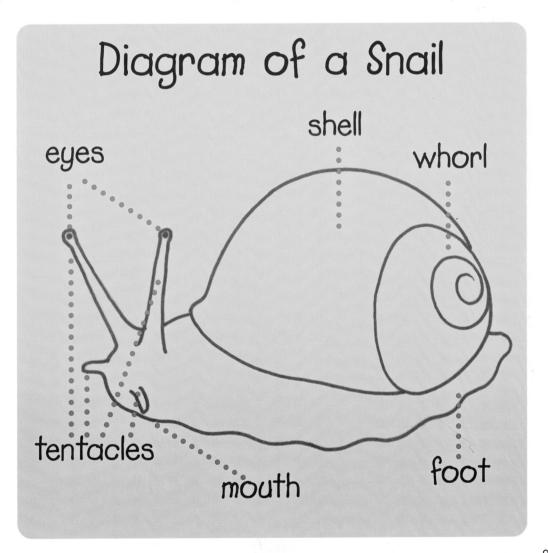

Diagram of a Snail

shell

eyes

whorl

tentacles

mouth

foot

What do snails eat?
We will find out.

The snail does not eat the lemon.

The snail eats the lettuce.
Lettuce helps it grow.

The snail eats chalk, too.
The chalk makes its shell hard.

Thursday

What do snails like?
My snail does not like sandpaper.
Snails like smooth paper.

My snail does not like
bright light.
Snails like cool, dark places.

We know how
to take care of snails.
We can take our snails home!